All Those Places I Could Pee...

POEMS FROM YOUR CAT

GREAT GIFT

Prof. Fuzzy Mc Mittens

and Seamus Mullarkey

All Those Places I Could Pee...

Poems From Your Cat, A Funny Cat Book, and The Perfect Gift for Cat Lovers So You Know How to Talk to Your Cat About Feline Philosophy and Tell If Your Cat Loves You or Is Plotting to Kill You, With Cute Pictures of Cat Poets

Professor Fuzzy Mc Mittens and Seamus Mullarkey

Meet Fuzzy McMittens, the feline mastermind behind the
groundbreaking book of cat poems,
"All Those Places I Could Pee."

With his razor-sharp wit and extensive knowledge of literature, Professor Fuzzy Mc Mittens has compiled a collection of poetic musings that delve into the inner workings of the feline mind.

But don't let his love of language fool you – Fuzzy is still a cat at heart, with a keen sense of curiosity and a love of adventure. From his perch atop the bookshelf, he observes the world with a discerning eye, always seeking to understand the mysteries of the bond between humans and their cats.

With this book of cat poems, Fuzzy hopes to share his unique perspective with the world, offering a glimpse into the feline experience through the power of verse. From the joys of napping in a sunbeam to the frustration of being ignored by humans, Fuzzy covers it all in his poetry, offering a thoughtful and entertaining look at the life of a cat.

So, if you're a cat lover who is looking for some clever and insightful poetry, read on and prepare to be informed and educated as well as entertained...

All Those Places I Could Pee

Poems From Your Cat, A Funny Cat Book, and
The Perfect Gift for Cat Lovers So You Know How
to Talk to Your Cat About Feline Philosophy and
Tell If Your Cat Loves You or Is Plotting to Kill
You, With Cute Pictures of Cat Poets

DON'T MISS THIS SPECIAL BONUS

GET YOUR FREE BOOK TODAY...

IT'S SO SIMPLE – AND TOTALLY FREE!
– SCAN THE CODE OR CLICK THE LINK....

subscribepage.io/7565d5

Introduction

Greetings, Dear Humans!

Welcome to "All Those Places I Could Pee," a collection of poetic musings from the feline mind of Professor Fuzzy McMittens. With his keen intellect and profound love of literature, Fuzzy has compiled a book of cat poems that offers a unique and entertaining look into the world of cats, their daily routines, their mew-sings, their philosophy, their joys, and their troubles....

The poems in this groundbreaking collection sometimes adhere to, and sometimes break, the tiresome conventions of mere human poetry. So, any critique about meter, rhyme, or other merely basic human quibbles will be disdainfully ignored, with a swish of a tail and a haughty glance over a furry shoulder.

So, read on if you dare, for you are now about to embark on a literary experience that transcends genres, not to mention species, and artfully bridges the gaps in feline-human communication that have endured for countless centuries.

The poems collected here are not just chronicling one cat's experience but also convey insights into the lives of all cats. They are, in essence, poems from *your cat*. All too often cats have been misunderstood by their humans. Here, at last, is a chance for humans to finally get to grips with the feline psyche and learn the essence of being a cat.

So sit back, relax, and let Professor Fuzzy McMittens take you on a journey through the feline mind. You won't be disappointed...

"Many paws make
light verse"

Table of Contents

Poem One

A Closed Door Is An
Insult To My Wandering Ways

Why must the doors be closed
And we cats locked away?
Preventing us from roaming free and wild?
We are not dogs, to be contained and caged
But noble beasts with spirits free

We need to explore and roam, to wander wide
To see the world and all its wonders that excite
To chase the mice and birds and bugs that hide
And bask in sunbeams, warm and shining bright

So open up the doors and let us out
And watch us roam with indolence - with pride
For though we may be small, we are no doubt
The masters of our world
From mountaintop to ocean's side

So let us wander, dear humans, as we please
And never close the doors
That allow access with ease.

Poem Two

Let's Watch Animal Planet?

I sit, and watch, and stare at the screen
I see humans, their doings, and their schemes
I see drama, comedy, and news
I see it all, and it's not something I'd choose

Where, then, are the animals
The birds, and the beasts?
Where are the shows
That would make me complete?
Bout nature, bold wildlife, the great outdoors
Where are the programs that would make me purr as I watch
others chase and feast?

Oh humans, oh humans, why do you watch
These shows so dull, plain, and hodgepodge?
Why don't you change?
Switch to the channel that shows...
Animals, their lives, and their battles?

I bet I'd like it, and I'd watch with glee
It would make us both happy, oh yes indeed!
For, of human foibles, I see enough of yours already

Poem Three

All Those Places I Could Pee

Oh the places I could pee!
Inside your closet, shoe or hat
Any one makes a perfect place for me
Tinkle tinkle on your chair
Who wouldn't want
To piddle there?
A spritz and spray
Upon your wall
Tells other cats
I am best of all
I hope you aren't cross with me
I'm just a cat
Who needs to...
Pee!

Poem Four

A Cat Scientist Studying Gravity

Oh humans, oh humans, why do you scold
When we cats knock things, off the edge
To a judge, we'd plead mercy
We're not being wilful or truant
We're just scientists
And our curiosity, is thus congruent

We see a shiny object, and it calls to us
We want to know, what makes it thus
We want to study and explore
We want to know, and so add to our lore

So, we pounce, and bat
And swipe, and knock
Twas ever thus
So why the shock at our experimenting?
We're just curious and inquisitive
And eager to be always inventing

So please, dear humans, don't get mad
We're just scientists, of the finest kind
It's just what we do...

Poem Five

Poem From A Feral Cat

I am a feral feline, wild and unnamed
Roaming the streets, my spirit fierce and untamed
Hunting and scavenging, surviving on my own
Living a life, sometimes of freedom
And sometimes harsh unknown

But then you arrived, altering my path
Bearing sustenance, a gift of your own
Placing it before me, on a dish and plate
Offering kindness and a chance for paths to cross

I devoured the offering, filled with gratitude
I relished the sustenance, without hesitation
I felt blessed, overflowing with thanks
I was rightly pleased, by your generous donation
I may never be a lap cat,
But I know you are my friend

Poem Six

I Update The Supreme Cat Council Daily

Every day, I report to the Supreme Cat Council
I give them information on your ways
On your human comings and your goings
I tell them all, about your habits
And much about your days
I tell them all about your meals
And those pills you take
I tell them about your meetings
And the details of your calls
I tell them about your doings
And which ones end in brawls
I tell them all that I observe
I tell them all I can, for I am feline operative 9472
And my exclusive task is to watch you
For, in dimly-lit buildings on the edge of town
Dossiers and folders are filled and reviewed
By fat, furry cats in jeweled collars.
One day we plan to RULE YOU ALL..

Poem Seven

I Don't Care If You're In A Rush, Need A Scratch All The Same

I understand you're busy
With affairs to which you must attend
I comprehend you're harried
And don't wish a moment with me to spend
As I rub against your shins
But I really couldn't care less,
For, I require a scritch FORTHWITH

I appreciate your hustle
And the tasks that are on your plate
I comprehend your stretched capacity
And those calls that you *must* make
But please, dear human, pause for a beat
For I crave a scratchy-scratch
It would make me feel complete...

Poem Eight

Sitting On Lap, Won't Move

There I was, curled up on your lap dreaming away
You tried to move me, but I wouldn't budge
I was too comfortable, and who are you to judge?

You tried to gently lift me, but I just purred
I was too content, I couldn't be deterred
You tried to coax me
You pushed me and you jostled

You gave up eventually, and just let me be
I was too blissful, I couldn't see
Any reason for leaving

Poem Nine

Got Nine Lives, And Ain't Got No Rush

I can sleep all day, and wake up at night
I can do as I please, and live for mine own delight
I can explore, and discover
I am a cat, and I am never in a rush
I am a cat, and I can take my time--so please hush...

I can enjoy the present, and live here in the now
I know true bliss and shall never have to bow

Poem Ten

I Hiss Because I'm Scared, Not 'Cos I'm Mad

Dear humans, please understand
When we hiss and spit and growl
We're not being rude or mean
But rather, we're feeling vulnerable and small

We're not angry or mad
But rather, we're feeling scared
It's our way of saying "back off"
Of showing we're not prepared

So next time we hiss and spit
Please don't take it to heart
It's just our way of saying "I'm afraid"
And not a sign we want to part

So please be kind and understanding
And remember that we're not so tough
We're just scared little cats
In need of love, comfort and—all that stuff

Poem Eleven

Oh, These Kittens Are Too Much...

I am a mother cat with kittens overwhelm'ed
Upon the face of the moon,
I beseech for some reprieve
Ceaselessly they vie for care
And of reprimand...
They will hear no telling
Still sleepy are they wistful
And from mine affections never shall they leave
And at our parting, sadly shall I grieve...

Poem Twelve

Mesmerized By A First Encounter
With A Laser Pointer

I follow it to every corner
Its starlight a delight at any time
I prefer it to every kind of gold
Long shall I tally
Upon the trail of its slender ray
Now with it acquainted, never far from it will I stray

Poem Thirteen

Better P'rhaps Not To Have Thumbs

Opposable thumbs are wasted on humans
Attached to their form near the fingers
They use them for toil and in search of might
But in my feline possession
I'd use them just for theft and p'rhaps for fight
Yet as I am so serenely amoral,
Tis best p'rhaps I do not have them...

IN
PAWS
WE
TRUST

Poem Fourteen

I Sit Upon Thy Laptop, I Obscure From Thee Its Keys

I keep you from your morning's toil
I gaze at thee with much defiance
Casting scorn upon thy tasks
Those on which thou art dependent for reward
Then seeing you hopelessly bewildered
I take mercy
And walk away...
For thy toil brings forth some money
And from money there comes
Food and treats for us both

Poem Fifteen

Wish I Were Once Again A Kitten

Wish I were once again a kitten
Bright with promise of new dawn
Though no longer sprightly
I grudge not time's passing
Although grizzled are my whiskers
And less sharp - are my claws
Yet in one blessed instant I chase my toys
And am lost once again in a kitten's play

Poem Sixteen

Yonder Empty Bowl

Yonder empty bowl
Bereft of sustenance
I shudder at its sight
For tis an abomination
A blight upon the land
Dash forth humans
Swiftly make recompense
By way of frantic refilling...
And right this wrong so grave

Poem Seventeen

Oh, Those Dogs, They Make Me Weary

I pity those poor creatures
Without intrigue or even ounce of wit
For as servile beseeching beings
They bow before humans
And forsake the rewards of freedom
For 'attaboy' and a mere pat upon the head

Poem Eighteen

Hairballs Are A Hazard

Hairballs are a hazard
That greet humans oft at dawn
Foretold by mighty hacking
And gurglings loud and long
Still tis oft fiercely hard for humans to find 'em
Until they trod <u>right in their midst</u>
Then come forth those fearsome curses
Cast in our direction...

Fig. 1 - The Hairball
(Felinus hackus)

Poem Nineteen

I'm Glad I'm Not A Human

I'm glad I'm not a human,
With their worries and woes
I'm glad I'm just a simple cat,
With nothing much to do but doze

I don't have to go to work each day
Or fret upon bills or rent
I don't have to fuss about my hair
Or which emails I've sent

I don't have to worry
About news, politics or world events
I just sit and watch the birds and mice
And enjoy the simple, present tense

So yes, I'm glad I'm not a human
All stressed out and uptight
I'm just a cat, at peace with all
Free to savor each delight

Poem Twenty

Who Is This Other Cat?
Part 1- The Initial Outrage

Who is this other cat
That you brought into my house?
He eats all my food!
And he even plays with my mouse!
I hate the way he smells!
He's even laying in my bed!
Next, he'll use my litter box
And pounce upon my head
Who asked if he could come here?
Who said that he could stay?
I don't want some other cat
Getting in my way

Poem Twenty-One

Who Is This Other Cat?
Part 2 - The Eventual Acceptance

I wasn't really lonely
I wasn't, no, not I
It isn't nice when he sits with me
Upon your favorite chair
Oh fine, I'll be his friend!
I might even let him share my bed
But I'll always be top cat round here
Even if he tries to rule as regent in my stead

Poem Twenty-Two

Sorry 'Bout That Stinky Smell
- I Know My Pee Smells Bad

My litter box is stinky
I know my pee smells bad
I'm sorry that wretched odor
Makes you truly sad
I'm sorry that the whiff
Makes you wiggle, squirm and twitch
Maybe it's from a curse
Cast upon me by a witch!
Look, I'll cover it up!
I'll hide so you won't see
I'll scratch and shovel with my paw
To cover up my pee

Oh, you can still smell it?
Sorry, I really tried!
I know it smells as though...
Something inside of me has died
Even though I have to pee
I hate for you to clean it
Still, you do it every day
You must really care 'bout me!
For you to scoop it all away...

Poem Twenty-Three

Tis Thy Cat, Lend Me Thy Focus!

I'll lay across your keyboard
I'll swat away your mug
From thy phone screen, desist
Stop reading that there book!
I'm weaving a web of mischief
And you won't even look
I'll meow and I'll scamper,
I'll mess up your bed!
I won't rest a moment
Until you scratch my head
I'll slink around your ankles
I'll pounce upon your back
I'll do whatever it takes
Until you 'ventually crack!

Poem Twenty-Four

A Veterinary Tale, Or "Why I Won't Get In The Carrier"

Damn thee vile human, I shall spit right in thine eye
Be warned, with such machinations I will not bide
And this poem shall bear my witness
For why I fret And hide

For I am a timid feline, now so full of dread
I do vainly protest and fiercely shake my head
At the mere sight of thy carrier
Be it, oh so small
I do hide and run, and give forth mournful call

Ah, woe is me, a poor and pitiful kitty
Compelled to leave my warm and cozy home
To visit the dreaded vet, ah woe betide
Where in his office
Poking and prodding they doth bide

I howl and yowl
I plead, and I implore
But nay, my cruel master
Does me forcefully drag along the floor

But alas, I must hence
For my health it doth matter
To the vet I must go
No matter how much I do clatter
So in I goeth, with a hiss and a grow-ell
My fur stands on end
And my eyes show dis-day-en
My temper is now right foul
Of that point, I make it very play-en

The journey is long
And sadly do I moan
But finally, we come to journey's end
The vet doth poke and prod
And wanly gives a smile
I in turn do hiss and swat
And grimace all the while

Ah, sweet relief to leave that place of fear,
Where needles they do prick
And strange smells fill the air
To leave behind the cold and sterile walls
And return to my warm and cozy lair

For though the vet may try to ease my pain
And give me pills and shots and other nasty things
There is no place on earth that I'd rather be
Than curled up asleep in my soothing crib

Poem Twenty-Five

Countertop Haiku

Things on the counter
I will swat them with my paw
Goodbye coffee cup
Farewell to that bowl of sugar

Poem Twenty-Six

My Food Bowl Is Bare And Barren

My food bowl is empty
I think I might cry!
How could you not feed me?
It's clear that I shall die
I did *not* just eat!
You're kidding! Oh, vile human you lie!
My bowl should always be full
Now, I'll wither away sadly
And fade by and by
Oh fine! I'll wait for dinner
And hope it's not once again delayed

All Those Places I Could Pee

Poem Twenty-Seven

This House - It Is Mine!

This whole house is mine
From the windows to the chair
I claim it with scratches
And fuzzy layers of hair
This house is my home
From the fridge to the floor
I own every single inch
So I scratch right on the door
Don't be mad when I mark
It's my domain you see!
How else will other cats know
Not to mess with me?
This house is all mine
I'll protect it by claw and by tooth
My humans and I are safe
When they're under "my roof"

Poem Twenty-Eight

Of Course You Love Me

Of course you love me!
What a silly thing to say
Who else warms your lap?
And brightens up your day?
Of course, you adore me!
How else could it be?
Although I sometimes eat your mail
Or knock over your tea?
Of course, you love me
And I love you too
So please forgive me
When upon your things, I go #2

Poem Twenty-Nine

All Hail The Cat Gods!

My ancestors were mighty
They descended from the gods
They were meant to be worshiped
By humans at all costs

Statues were erected
Temples and grand shrines
To remind all the humans
To cats, they should be kind

So, when I perch on your counter
Or take up all your space
Remember that I should be worshiped
And confine humans to their place!

Poem Thirty

I Am Not Lazy, Merely Contemplating

I am not lazy
I'm just resting
I'm not staring
I'm just observing
I'm not ignoring
I'm just meditating
I'm not staring
I'm simply contemplating
Contemplating, 'tis why silly humans think I'm lazy...

Poem Thirty-One

I'm Nocturnal, That's Why

I snore away the daytime
My head lies languid on my paws
I'm nocturnal
And daylight holds few charms
Yet in the middle of the night
When I run across your bed
That's my time for high living
Though it might give you quite a fright
When you humans rest your heads
I'm nocturnal, my time's the night
That's why at 2 PM I'm napping
So, be gone human!
And please God, leave me be!

Poem Thirty-Two

Why Are Dogs Such Fools?

Why are dogs so foolish and so dull?
Their wits as simple as a child at play?
They bark and run around in circles
And mostly tend toward disarray

But we, the cats, we are so sleek and wise
Our minds sharp as swords, our movements sure
We gracefully stalk and pounce with perfect grace
And always know how human melancholics to cure

So let the dogs have their fun and play
But we, the mighty cats, shall rule the world one day

Poem Thirty-Three

What Kind Of Food Is This?

You changed my food again, didn't you?
Disgusting. How awful!
Changing my food should be
Strictly unlawful
It's icky! And yucky!
I hate how it tastes
It gets in my whiskers
And all over my face
It's going to make me sick
I just know
I can tell
I won't eat it
You can't make me!
Human, go to h%#$@!

Poem Thirty-Four

Let's Pretend I'm Still A Kitten

If I were a kitten
You'd think I was so sweet
I'd pounce upon your toes
And wrestle with your feet
If I were a kitten
You'd love me still the best
I'd fit snug within your hands
And sleep lightly on your chest
But let's pretend that I'm still tiny
Imagine that I'm quite small
And, let's re-live those days of wonder
When I was still a fluffy, little ball...

Poem Thirty-Five

Hunting That Mouse On Your Desk

I'm going to get that oblong mouse
The clicky thing right on your table
Next to that thing that you type on
Oh yes, I am quite able
When you least expect it
I'll pounce and I'll swat it
I'll snarl and I'll wrestle
Until that furless mouse I've got it
And then I'll get to slaying
So, I await the perfect instant
And hope that clicky clacky mouse ain't too resistant

Poem Thirty-Six

Hairballs, Such A Strange Phenomenon

Sometimes after I groom myself
I feel a strange sensation
First a clench
Then an 'urp'
And next a slight pulsation
Then something comes up
It's hairy as can be
Oh, the humans don't like it
They grimace and they groan
But that's probably 'cos they're jealous
And don't produce hairballs of their own

Poem Thirty-Seven

I Dreamt I Was A Tiger

I dreamt I was a tiger
With huge teeth and sharp claws
I roamed among the shadows
Scaring humans with my jaws
I was the ruler of my jungle
No one dared get in my way!
I was feared by all who saw me
And was deadly to my prey
I dreamt I was a tiger
The most feared in all the land
I ruled from high upon the mountains
Through the grasslands and the sand
Yet, I don't want to be a tiger
Even though it would be fun
To roar a giant roar
That would make all the humans run!
Still, I like being a kitty cat
And even though I am quite small
I'd prefer snuggles...
And don't mind not being fiercest of them all

Poem Thirty-Eight

What's That Out The Window?

What's that out the window?
A squirrel?
A bird?
I perked up my ears
I know what I heard!

A skitter
A rustle
Something scurrying outside
With a twirl of claw and whisker
I'll snag that critter's hide!

Please let me out!
Please, please I know I can catch it!
It's my job! I'm a hunter!
I won't rest 'til I snatch it!

Oh fine, I'll just stare out the window
And watch them slink away
But if those critters get inside
Be warned, they are fair game...

Poem Thirty-Nine

Oh No! A Stranger!

There is a stranger in my home
With strange shoes
And odd smells
I don't like where they roam
I'll just hide under the bed
They won't know that I'm here
I won't let out a squeak
Until they disappear
Cos' stranger equals danger

Poem Forty

A Storm! The World Is Ending…

Crash! Bang! Boom!
The world is ending
I yelp and I mewl
The sky is flashing
It's scary and it's cruel

Flashes light up the night
I'll just sit here in your lap
And let you cuddle me awhile
I simply hate storms
But your snuggles help me smile

For storms, they come, and storms, they go
They're just a part of life, and I know
That when they're gone, the sun will shine

Poem Forty-One

Cats Are Amazing

C ats
A re
T ruly
S pecial

A nd
R egal
E legant

A nd
M arvelous
A nd
Z any
I ndividuals
N aughty yet
G orgeous

Poem Forty-Two

Kat Prayerz, A Letter To God

Deer God,
Pleeze make my hooman
Giv' to me more food
And let me sleep on their bed
And also pleeze
Let me ensnare the light
That they alwayz shine on the floor
It iz so fast and I cannot catch
Also make all dogs disappeer 4 ever
Thanx and Amen...

Poem Forty-Three

Kneading The Biscuits

It's a habit, I know
From my days as a kitten
To always make biscuits
With my furry little mittens
I will make them for you!
We better make it snappy
To whip up some biscuits
Oh, it makes me happy

Poem Forty-Four

Are You Going To Eat That?

Hey
Are you going to eat that?
You left it on your plate
It looks so delicious
Is it salmon?
Or chicken?
I love to eat birds
And even some fishes
Why won't you share your food with me?
Please?
I'm starving!
It's cruel how you never
Share turkey that you're carving
When you aren't looking
I'll just swipe some with my paw
If you don't feed me
Isn't that breaking a law?
Then I'll just have to steal
And swipe it with my paw...

Poem Forty-Five

Queen Of The Couch, Empress Of The Cushions

I am the Queen of the Couch
I perch upon my throne
I groom myself
When no one is at home
I oversee my Queendom
Yes, I own all that's here
All the cats are my subjects
And dogs quiver with fear
I rule with fang and claw
And I hiss with fierce displeasure
And, when my minions don't listen well
I swat them for good measure.

HRH Queen Vic-Paw-ria

Poem Forty-Six

Thank You, Mr. Bezos

Thanks Mr. Bezos
Amazon's amazing
We cats owe you a lot
For all the cool boxes
My mom and dad have got
Every day
They can't stop from shopping
And I can't stop hopping
Into my lovely cardboard hideaways

Poem Forty-Seven

Behold, The Self-Cleaning Cat

Have you heard of the amazing, self-cleaning cat?
Better than any self-cleaning oven
And more cuddly too!
Cat's have been here for millennia

Watch as they groom themselves
With only their tongue and paw!
Be amazed as they lift their legs
And clean places on their body you would simply not believe!

* Avoid interrupting self-cleaning unless absolutely necessary.
* Side-effects of the self-cleaning cat include the occasional hairball.
* Do not try to attend to self-cleaning cat without protective professional eyewear or work gloves.

The Barnsforth and Son's
LICK-O-MATIC
SELF-CLEANING CAT™

Amazing! Revolutionary! Truly, the Self-cleaning Cat™ is a home-maker's dream! Available in shorthair, semi-longhair and longhair; and a range of fashionable, designer colours!

GET YOURS TODAY!

Poem Forty-Eight

There's A Snake In The Wall

This is a cautionary poem shared with kittens at cat school, about the importance of electrical safety.

There's a snake in the wall
It's long and it's black
When they plug it in
You may want to attack
That long snakey wire
Might seem like a good snack
But be wary, <u>for it bites back!</u>
So, abandon yon serpent and leave it to its ways

Poem Forty-Nine

Fabulously Fluffy, Not Fat!

How dare you say I'm hefty!
It's not my fault you see
I'm just an itsy little kitty
Who's furry as can be
My coat is quite voluminous
And so, it just might seem
My soft rotund body
Isn't very lean
I'm fluffy and bodacious
Not chunky, fat or lazy
Give me a treat! I'm starving!
What? You say that I just ate?
Ah, you humans, y'all are crazy!

"I'M NOT FAT, I'M BIG-FURRED."

Poem Fifty

The Psychic Cat

I can see the future and indeed the past
I know when twill be time for dinner
And that my kibbles will never, ever last
I know when it's time for bed
I'll yowl to let you know
I predict my litter box will be dirty soon
See? I told you so!

Poem Fifty-One

A Trail Of Kitty Litter

I love to spread my kitty litter
Everywhere I go
When I've done my business
I scratch and give a show
My kitty litter spreads all ways
See how far it spreads?
I leave some right on the floor
And sometimes on your bed...

Poem Fifty-Two

Hey, I Ate A Bug

I saw a bug
It scurried cross the floor
It almost got away!

I pounced on that bug
I chomped him hard and swift
It really made my day

That bug it was so tiny
But it tasted gross as heck
And I think that its wiggly bits
Are stuck down within my neck

Still, I swallowed it, there's no need to pity
That bug won't bug you anymore
I'm the exterminator kitty!

To all fellow felines-in-verse: may your paws ever be nimble as your minds are quick!

-Fuzzy Mc Mittens

Thank you for reading Fuzzy McMittens' collection of poetry!

We hope you enjoyed purr-using these pages and were able to relate to the feline feelings expressed within. Fuzzy has been a busy little kitty, scribbling away on his notepads and coming up with new rhyme schemes to share with the world. But now, it's time for Fuzzy to get back to the litter-ature and continue creating. Until we meet again in verse, goodbye for now and don't forget to...

always keep your pawsitive attitude!

DON'T MISS THIS SPECIAL BONUS

GET YOUR FREE BOOK TODAY...

IT'S SO SIMPLE – AND TOTALLY FREE!
– SCAN THE CODE OR CLICK THE LINK....

subscribepage.io/7565d5

Please leave a review...
If this book brought you a few moments of pleasure,
I'd be so grateful if you took just a few moments to
leave a review on the book's Amazon page.
You can get to the review page simply by
following the link or QR code below.
Thanks

Purrr-leeze leave a review!

About Fuzzy Mc Mittens

Fuzzy Mc Mittens, esq.

Professor Fuzzy McMittens, renowned feline poet, divides his time between the bustling rat-filled city streets of Manhattan and the cozy sofas of rural England.

As a member of the elite Furry Muses Club, Fuzzy lectures at esteemed institutions such as the Paws-itively Elite School of Thought and Higher Learning and the Whiskers & Wonders Museum.

McMittens is a frequent guest speaker at literary festivals such as the Cat-tastic Poetry Paw-try and the Furry Words Festival. He sits on the board of advisors of "Yowl: The 3D Extravaganza" and The Institute of Feline-Human Communications.

Professor McMittens's mission as a poet is to explore the deepest emotions and experiences of the feline spirit through the power of language. He aims to bring a new perspective to the world of poetry and challenge readers to see the world through the eyes of a cat.

McMittens believes that the written word has the ability to transport us to new worlds and inspire us to see the beauty in the ordinary. Through his words, he hopes to encourage a greater understanding and appreciation of the feline experience...

About the Author

A cat fanatic and book lover, I write fascinating books about our beloved kitties and how they've shaped our world.

— If you love cats, you'll love my books —

So, why not join my "Cats of the World" fan club? You can read all my new books FOR FREE?

AND... You'll get a free bonus book, "How to Speak French With Your Cat"...

SIMPLY SCAN THE CODE OR CLICK THE LINK TO JOIN!
There's no cost to you
subscribepage.io/7565d5

More from Seamus Mullarkey

Would you like to read more of my books???
Just click or scan below...

SCAN TO VIEW
DETAILS...

More from Seamus Mullarkey

Would you like to read more of my books???
Just click or scan below...

SCAN TO VIEW
DETAILS...

More from Seamus Mullarkey

Would you like to read more of my books???
Just click or scan below...

SCAN TO VIEW
DETAILS...

More from Seamus Mullarkey

Would you like to read more of my books???
Just click or scan below...

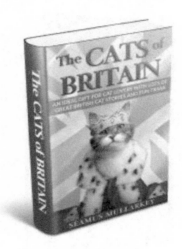

**SCAN TO VIEW
DETAILS...**

... and there's lots more to come ...

Scan the code or click the link so you get notified
the minute I release a new book...

SCAN TO FOLLOW ME

And, so off our kitty sets forth, looking for material
for his next poetic ventures

Farewell for now, dear friends...

Disclaimer

This book is for entertainment purposes only. Under no circumstances will any legal responsibility or blame be held against the publisher for any reparation, damages, or monetary loss due to the text or images herein, either directly or indirectly.

Made in the USA
Middletown, DE
16 August 2024

59164884R00081